HARVARD BUSINESS REVIEW
CLASSICS

BLUE OCEAN LEADERSHIP

W. Chan Kim and
Renée Mauborgne

Harvard Business Review Press
Boston, Massachusetts

Copyright 2017 Harvard Business School Publishing Corporation
Originally published in *Harvard Business Review* in May 2014
Reprint #R1405C
All rights reserved

Printed in the United States of America

10 9 8 7 6 5 4 3 2 1

No part of this publication may be reproduced, stored in or introduced into a retrieval system, or transmitted, in any form, or by any means (electronic, mechanical, photocopying, recording, or otherwise), without the prior permission of the publisher. Requests for permission should be directed to permissions@hbsp.harvard.edu, or mailed to Permissions, Harvard Business School Publishing, 60 Harvard Way, Boston, Massachusetts 02163.

The web addresses referenced in this book were live and correct at the time of the book's publication but may be subject to change.

Cataloging-in-Publication data is forthcoming.

ISBN: 978-1-63369-264-0
eISBN: 978-1-63369-265-7

The paper used in this publication meets the requirements of the American National Standard for Permanence of Paper for Publications and Documents in Libraries and Archives Z39.48-1992.

BLUE OCEAN LEADERSHIP

THE HARVARD BUSINESS REVIEW CLASSICS SERIES

Since 1922, *Harvard Business Review* has been a leading source of breakthrough ideas in management practice—many of which still speak to and influence us today. The HBR Classics series now offers you the opportunity to make these seminal pieces a part of your permanent management library. Each volume contains a groundbreaking idea that has shaped best practices and inspired countless managers around the world—and will change how you think about the business world today.

BLUE OCEAN
LEADERSHIP

It's a sad truth about the workplace: just 30% of employees are actively committed to doing a good job. According to Gallup's 2013 *State of the American Workplace* report, 50% of employees merely put their time in, while the remaining 20% act out their discontent in counterproductive ways, negatively influencing their coworkers, missing days on the job, and driving customers away through poor service. Gallup estimates that the 20% group alone costs the

US economy around half a trillion dollars each year.

What's the reason for the widespread employee disengagement? According to Gallup, poor leadership is a key cause.

Most executives—not just those in America—recognize that one of their biggest challenges is closing the vast gulf between the potential and the realized talent and energy of the people they lead. As one CEO put it, "We have a large workforce that has an appetite to do a good job up and down the ranks. If we can transform them—tap into them through effective leadership—there will be an awful lot of people out there doing an awful lot of good."

Of course, managers don't intend to be poor leaders. The problem is that they lack a clear understanding of just what changes it would take to bring out the best in everyone and achieve high impact. We believe that leaders can obtain this understanding through an approach we call "blue ocean leadership." It draws on our research on blue ocean strategy, our model for creating new market space by converting noncustomers into customers, and applies its concepts and analytic frameworks to help leaders release the blue ocean of unexploited talent and energy in their organizations—rapidly and at low cost.

The underlying insight is that leadership, in essence, can be thought of as a service that people in an organization "buy" or "don't buy." Every leader in that sense has customers: the bosses to whom the leader must deliver performance, and the followers who need the leader's guidance and support to achieve. When people value your leadership practices, they in effect buy your leadership. They're inspired to excel and act with commitment. But when employees don't buy your leadership, they disengage, becoming noncustomers of your leadership. Once we started thinking about leadership in this way, we began to see that the concepts and frameworks we were developing to create new demand by converting noncustomers into customers could be adapted to help leaders convert disengaged employees into engaged ones.

Over the past 10 years we and Gavin Fraser, a Blue Ocean Strategy Network expert, have interviewed hundreds of people in organizations to understand where leadership was falling short and how it could be transformed while conserving leaders' most precious resource: time. In this article we present the results of our research.

KEY DIFFERENCES FROM CONVENTIONAL LEADERSHIP APPROACHES

Blue ocean leadership rapidly brings about a step change in leadership strength. It's distinct from traditional leadership development approaches in several overarching ways. Here are the three most salient:

Focus on acts and activities

Over many years a great deal of research has generated insights into the values, qualities, and behavioral styles that make for good leadership, and these have formed the basis of development programs and executive coaching. The implicit assumption is that changes in values, qualities, and behavioral styles ultimately translate into high performance.

But when people look back on these programs, many struggle to find evidence of notable change. As one executive put it, "Without years of dedicated efforts, how can you transform a person's character or behavioral traits? And can you really measure and assess whether leaders are embracing and internalizing these personal traits and styles? In theory, yes, but in reality it's hard at best."

Blue ocean leadership, by contrast, focuses on *what acts and activities leaders need to undertake* to boost their teams' motivation and business results, not on *who leaders need to be*. This difference in emphasis is important.

It is markedly easier to change people's acts and activities than their values, qualities, and behavioral traits. Of course, altering a leader's activities is not a complete solution, and having the right values, qualities, and behavioral traits matters. But activities are something that any individual can change, given the right feedback and guidance.

Connect closely to market realities

Traditional leadership development programs tend to be quite generic and are often detached from what firms stand for in the eyes of customers and from the market results people are expected to achieve. In contrast, under blue ocean leadership, the people who face market realities are asked for their direct input on how their leaders hold them back and what those leaders could do to help them best serve customers and other key stakeholders. And when people are engaged in defining the leadership practices that will enable them to thrive, and *those practices are connected to the market realities* against which they need to perform, they're highly motivated to create the best possible profile for leaders and to make the new solutions work. Their willing cooperation maximizes the acceptance of new profiles for leadership while minimizing implementation costs.

Distribute leadership across all management levels

Most leadership programs focus on executives and their potential for impact now and in the future. But the key to a successful organization is having empowered leaders at every level, because outstanding organizational performance often comes down to the motivation and actions of middle and frontline leaders, who are in closer contact with the market. As one senior executive put it, "The truth is that we, the top management, are not in the field to fully appreciate the middle and frontline actions. We need effective leaders at every level to maximize corporate performance."

Blue ocean leadership is designed to be applied across the three distinct management levels: *top, middle*, and *frontline*. It calls for profiles for leaders that are tailored to the very different tasks, degrees of power, and environments you find at each level. Extending leadership capabilities deep into the front line unleashes the latent talent and drive of a critical mass of employees, and creating strong distributed leadership significantly enhances performance across the organization.

THE FOUR STEPS OF BLUE OCEAN LEADERSHIP

Now let's walk through how to put blue ocean leadership into practice. It involves four steps.

1. See your leadership reality

A common mistake organizations make is to discuss changes in leadership before resolving differences of opinion over what leaders are actually doing. Without a common understanding of where leadership stands and is falling short, a forceful case for change cannot be made.

Achieving this understanding is the objective of the first step. It takes the form of what we call as-is Leadership Canvases, analytic visuals that show just how managers at each level invest their time and effort, as perceived by the customers of their leadership. An organization begins the process by creating a canvas for each of its three management levels.

A team of 12 to 15 senior managers is typically selected to carry out this project. The people chosen should cut across functions and be recognized as good leaders in the company so that the team has immediate credibility. The team is then broken into three smaller subteams, each focused on one level and charged with interviewing its relevant leadership customers—both bosses and subordinates—and ensuring that a representative number of each are included.

The aim is to uncover how people experience current leadership and to start a companywide conversation about what leaders do and should do at each level. The customers of leaders are asked which acts and activities—good and bad—their leaders spend most of their time on, and which are key to motivation and performance but are neglected by their leaders. Getting at the specifics is important; the as-is canvases must be grounded in acts and activities that reflect each level's specific market reality and performance goals. This involves a certain amount of probing.

At a company we'll call British Retail Group (BRG), many interviewees commented that middle managers spent much of their time playing politics. The subteam focused on that level pushed for clarification and discovered that two acts principally accounted for this judgment. One was that the leaders tended to divide responsibility among people, which created uncertainty about accountability—and some internal competitiveness. The result was a lot of finger-pointing and the perception that the leaders were playing people against one another. The subteam also found that the leaders spent much of their time in meetings with senior management. This led subordinates to conclude that their leaders were more interested in maximizing political "face time" and spinning news than in being present to support them.

After four to six weeks of interviews, subteam members come together to create as-is Leadership Profiles by pooling their findings and determining, based on frequency of citation, the dominant leadership acts and activities at each level. To help the subteams focus on what really matters, we typically ask for no more than 10 to 15 leadership acts and activities per level. These get registered on the horizontal axis of the as-is canvas, and the extent to which leaders do them is registered on the vertical axis. The cap of 10 to 15 prevents the canvas from becoming a statement of everything and nothing.

The result is almost always eye-opening. It's not uncommon to find that 20% to 40% of the acts and activities of leaders at all three levels provide only questionable value to those above and below them. It's also not uncommon to find that leaders are underinvesting in 20% to 40% of the acts and activities that interviewees at their level cite as important.

At BRG, the canvas for senior managers revealed that their customers thought they spent most of their time on essentially middle-management acts and activities, while the canvas of middle managers indicated that they seemed to be absorbed in protecting bureaucratic procedures. Frontline leaders were seen to be focused on trying to keep their bosses happy by doing things like deferring customer queries to them, which satisfied their desire to be in control. When we asked team members to describe each canvas in a tagline, an exercise that's part of the process, they labeled the frontline Leadership Profile "Please the Boss," the middle-manager profile "Control and Play Safe," and the senior manager profile "Focus on the Day-to-Day." (For an example, see the exhibit "What middle managers actually do.")

The implications were depressing. The biggest "aha" for the subteams was that senior managers appeared to have scarcely any time to do the real job of top management—thinking, probing, identifying opportunities on the horizon, and gearing up the organization to capitalize on them. Faced with firsthand, repeated evidence of the shortcomings of leadership practices, the subteams could not defend the current Leadership Profiles. The canvases made a strong case for change at all three levels; it was clear that people throughout the organization wished for it.

2. Develop alternative Leadership Profiles

At this point the subteams are usually eager to explore what effective Leadership Profiles would look like at each level. To achieve this, they go back to their interviewees with two sets of questions.

The first set is aimed at pinpointing the extent to which each act and activity on the canvas is either a cold spot (absorbing leaders' time but adding little or no value) or a hot spot (energizing employees and inspiring them to apply their talents, but currently underinvested in by leaders or not addressed at all).

The second set prompts interviewees to think beyond the bounds of the company and focus on effective leadership acts they've observed outside the organization, in particular those that could have a strong impact if adopted by internal leaders at their level. Here fresh ideas emerge about what

leaders could be doing but aren't. This is
not, however, about benchmarking against
corporate icons; employees' personal expe-
riences are more likely to produce insights.
Most of us have come across people in our
lives who have had a disproportionately
positive influence on us. It might be a sports
coach, a schoolteacher, a scoutmaster, a
grandparent, or a former boss. Whoever
those role models are, it's important to get
interviewees to detail which acts and activities they believe would add real value for
them if undertaken by their current leaders.

To process the findings from the second round of interviews, the subteams
apply an analytic tool we call the Blue
Ocean Leadership Grid (see the table by

the same name). For each leadership level the interview results get incorporated into this grid. Typically, we start with the cold-spot acts and activities, which go into the Eliminate or Reduce quadrants depending on how negatively interviewees judge them. This energizes the subteams right away, because people immediately perceive the benefits of stopping leaders from doing things that add little or no value. Cutting back on those activities also gives leaders the time and space they need to raise their game. Without that breathing room, a step change in leadership strength would remain largely wishful thinking, given leaders' already full plates. From the cold spots we move to the hot spots, which go into the Raise quadrant if they involve current acts and activities or Create for those not currently performed at all by leaders. With this input, the subteams draft two to four "to-be" canvases for each leadership level. These analytic visuals illustrate Leadership Profiles that can lift individual and organizational performance, and juxtapose them against the as-is Leadership Profiles. The subteams produce a range of leadership models, rather than stop at one set of possibilities, to thoroughly explore new leadership space.

3. Select to-be Leadership Profiles

After two to three weeks of drawing and redrawing their Leadership Canvases, the subteams present them at what we call a "leadership fair." Fair attendees include board members and top, middle, and front-line managers.

The event starts with members of the original senior team behind the effort describing the process and presenting the three as-is canvases. With those three visuals, the team establishes why change is necessary, confirms that comments from interviewees at all levels were taken into account, and sets the context against which the to-be Leadership Profiles can be understood and appreciated. Although the as-is canvases often present a sobering reality, as they did at BRG, the Leadership Profiles are shown and discussed only at the aggregate level. That makes individual leaders more open to change, because they feel that everyone is in the same boat.

With the stage set, the subteams present the to-be profiles, hanging their canvases on the walls so that the audience can easily see them. Typically, the subteam that focused on frontline leaders will go first. After the presentation, the attendees are each given three Post-it notes and told to put one next to their favorite Leadership Profile. And if they find that canvas especially compelling, they can put up to three Post-its on it.

After all the votes are in, the company's senior executives probe the attendees about why they voted as they did. The same process is then repeated for the two other leadership levels. (We find it easier to deal with each level separately and sequentially, and that doing so increases voters' recall of the discussion.)

{ 23 }

After about four hours everyone in attendance has a clear picture of the current Leadership Profile of each level, the completed Blue Ocean Leadership Grids, and a selection of to-be Leadership Profiles that could create a significant change in leadership performance. Armed with this information and the votes and comments of attendees, the top managers convene outside the fair room and decide which to-be Leadership Profile to move forward on at each level. Then they return and explain their decisions to the fair's participants.

At BRG, more than 125 people voted on the profiles, and fair attendees greeted the three that were selected with enthusiasm. The tagline for frontline leaders' to-be profile was "Cut Through the Crap." (Sadly, this was later refined to "Cut Through to Serve Customers.") In this profile, frontline leaders did not defer the vast majority of customer queries to middle management and spent less time jumping through procedural hoops. Their time was directed to training frontline personnel to deliver on company promises on the spot, resolve customer problems, quickly help customers in distress, and make meaningful cross-sales— leadership acts and activities that fired up the frontline workers, were sure to excite customers, and would have a direct impact on the company's bottom line.

"Liberate, Coach, and Empower" was the tagline for middle management's to-be profile. Here leaders' time and attention shifted from controlling to supporting employees.

This involved eliminating and reducing a range of oversight activities—such as requiring weekly reports on customer calls received and funds spent on office supplies— that sapped people's energy and kept front-line leaders at their desks. The profile also included new actions aimed at managing, disseminating, and integrating the knowledge of frontline leaders and their staff. In practical terms, this meant spending much more time providing face-to-face coaching and feedback.

The tagline for the to-be profile of senior management was "Delegate and Chart the Company's Future." With the acts and activities of frontline and middle managers reset, senior managers would be freed up to devote a significant portion of their time to thinking about the big picture—the changes in the industry and their implications for strategy and the organization. They would spend less time putting out fires.

The board members who attended the leadership fair felt strongly that the to-be Leadership Profiles supported the interests of customers as well as shareholders' profit and growth objectives. The frontline leaders were energized and ready to charge ahead. Senior managers went from feeling towed under the waves by all the middle-management duties they had to coordinate and attend to, to feeling as if they could finally get their heads above water and see the beauty of the ocean they had to chart.

The trickiest to-be Leadership Profile was middle management's. Letting go of control and empowering the people below them can be tough for folks in this organizational tier. But the to-be Leadership Profiles of both frontline and senior management helped clear the path to change at this level.

4. Institutionalize new leadership practices

After the fair is over, the original subteam members communicate the results to the people they interviewed who were not at the fair.

Organizations then distribute the agreed-on to-be profiles to the leaders at each level. The subteam members hold meetings with leaders to walk them through their canvases, explaining what should be eliminated, reduced, raised, and created. This step reinforces the buy-in that the initiative has been building by briefing leaders throughout the organization on key findings at each step of the process and tapping many of them for input. And because every leader is in effect the buyer of another level of leadership, all managers will be working to change, knowing that their bosses will be doing the same thing on the basis of input they directly provided.

The leaders are then charged with passing the message along to their direct reports and explaining to them how the new Leadership Profiles will allow them to be more effective. To keep the new profiles top of mind, the to-be canvases are pinned up prominently in the offices of both the leaders and their reports. Leaders are tasked with holding regular monthly meetings at which they gather their direct reports' feedback on how well they're making the transition to the new profiles. All comments must be illustrated with specific examples. Has the leader cut back on the acts and activities that were to be eliminated and reduced in the new Leadership Profile? If yes, how? If not, in what instances was she still engaging in them? Likewise, is she focusing more on what does add value and doing the new activities in her profile? Though the meetings can be unnerving at first—both for employees who have to critique the boss and for the bosses whose actions are being exposed to scrutiny—it doesn't take long before a team spirit and mutual respect take hold, as all people see how the changes in leadership are positively influencing their performance.

Through the changes highlighted by the to-be profiles, BRG was able to deepen its leadership strength and achieve high impact at lower cost. Consider the results produced just at the frontline level: Turnover of BRG's 10,000-plus frontline employees dropped from about 40% to 11% in the first year, reducing both recruitment and training costs by some 50%. The total savings, including those from decreased absenteeism, amounted to more than $50 million that year. On top of that, BRG's customer satisfaction scores climbed by over 30%, and leaders at all levels reported feeling less stressed, more energized by their ability to act, and more confident that they were making a greater contribution to the company, customers, and their own personal development.

EXECUTION IS BUILT INTO THE FOUR STEPS

Any change initiative faces skepticism. Think of it as the "bend over—here it comes again" syndrome. While blue ocean leadership also meets such a reaction initially, it counters it by building good execution into the process. The four steps are founded on the principles of fair process: engagement, explanation, and expectation clarity. The power of these principles cannot be overstated, and we have

written extensively about their impact on
the quality of execution for over 20 years.
(See, for example, our article "Fair Process:
Managing in the Knowledge Economy,"
HBR, July–August 1997.)

In the leadership development context, the application of fair process
achieves buy-in and ownership of the to-be
Leadership Profiles and builds trust, pre-
paring the ground for implementation. The
principles are applied in a number of ways,
with the most important practices being:

- *Respected senior managers spearhead
  the process.* Their engagement is not
  ceremonial; they conduct interviews
  and draw the canvases. This strongly
  signals the importance of the initiative,

which makes people at all levels feel respected and gives senior managers a visceral sense of what actions are needed to create a step change in leadership performance. Here's a typical employee reaction: "At first, I thought this was just one of those initiatives where management loves to talk about the need for change but then essentially goes back to doing what they've always done. But when I saw that leading senior managers were driving the process and rolling up their sleeves to push the change, I thought to myself, 'Hmm . . . they may just finally mean it.'"

- *People are engaged in defining what leaders should do.* Since the to-be profiles are generated with the employees' own input, people have confidence in the changes made. The process also makes them feel more deeply engaged with their leaders, because they have greater ownership of what their leaders are doing. Here's what people told us: "Senior management said they were going to come and talk to people at all levels to understand what we need our leaders to do and not do, so we could thrive. And I thought, 'I'll believe it when someone comes knocking on my door.' And then they knocked."

- *People at all levels have a say in the final decision.* A slice of the organization across the three management levels gets to vote in selecting the new Leadership Profiles. Though the top managers have the final say on the to-be profiles and may not choose those with the most votes, they are required to provide a clear, sound explanation for their decisions in front of all attendees. Here's some typical feedback: "The doubts we had that our comments were just paid lip service to were dispelled when we saw how our inputs were figured into the to-be profiles. We realized then that our voices were heard."

- *It's easy to assess whether expectations are being met.* Clarity about what needs to change to move from the as-is to the to-be Leadership Profiles makes it simple to monitor progress. The monthly review meetings between leaders and their direct reports help the organization check whether it's making headway. We've found that those meetings keep leaders honest, motivate them to continue with change, and build confidence in both the process and the sincerity of the leaders. By collecting feedback from those meetings, top management can assess how rapidly leaders are making the shift from their as-is to their to-be Leadership Profiles, which becomes a key input in annual performance evaluations. This is what people say: "With the one-page visual of our old and new Leadership Profiles, we can easily track the progress in moving from the old to the new. In it, everyone can see with clarity precisely where we are in closing the gap."

Essentially, the gift that fair process confers is trust and, hence, voluntary cooperation, a quality vital to the leader-follower relationship. Anyone who has ever worked in an organization understands how important trust is. If you trust the process and the people you work for, you're willing to go the extra mile and give your best. If you don't trust them, you'll stick to the letter of the law that binds your contract with the organization and devote your energy to protecting your position and fighting over turf rather than to winning customers and creating value. Not only will your abilities be wasted, but they will often work against your organization's performance.

BECOMING A BLUE OCEAN LEADER

We never cease to be amazed by the talent and energy we see in the organizations we study. Sadly, we are equally amazed by how much of it is squandered by poor leadership. Blue ocean leadership can help put an end to that.

The Leadership Canvases give people a concrete, visual framework in which they can surface and discuss the improvements leaders need to make. The fairness of the process makes the implementation and monitoring of those changes far easier than in traditional top-down approaches. Moreover, blue ocean leadership achieves a transformation with less time and effort, because leaders are not trying to alter who they are and break the habits of a lifetime. They are simply changing the tasks they carry out. Better yet, one of the strengths of blue ocean leadership is its scalability. You don't have to wait for your company's top leadership to launch this process. Whatever management level you belong to, you can awaken the sleeping potential of your people by taking them through the four steps.

Are you ready to be a blue ocean leader?

TABLE 1

The Blue Ocean Leadership Grid

The Blue Ocean Leadership Grid is an analytic tool that challenges people to think about which acts and activities leaders should do less of because they hold people back, and which leaders should do more of because they inspire people to give their all. Current activities from the leaders' "as-is" profiles (which may add value or not), along with new activities that employees believe would add a lot of value if leaders started doing them, are assigned to the four categories in the grid. Organizations then use the grids to develop new profiles of effective leadership.

Eliminate	Reduce	Raise	Create
What acts and activities do leaders invest their time and intelligence in that should be eliminated?	What acts and activities do leaders invest their time and intelligence in that should be reduced well below their current level?	What acts and activities do leaders invest their time and intelligence in that should be raised well above their current level?	What acts and activities should leaders invest their time and intelligence in that they currently don't undertake?

What middle managers actually do

As-is Leadership Canvases show the activities that employees see leaders engaging in, and the amount of time and energy they think leaders spend on each. The canvas below, for middle managers at the retail company BRG, reveals that people viewed them as rule enforcers who played it safe.

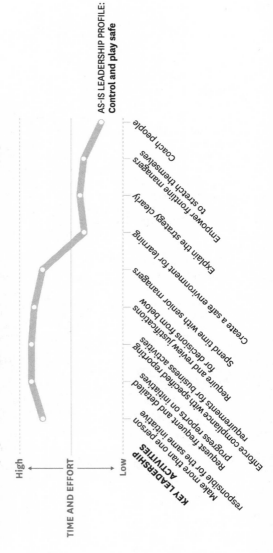

AS-IS LEADERSHIP PROFILE: Control and play safe

TIME AND EFFORT — High / Low

KEY LEADERSHIP ACTIVITIES

- Make more than one person responsible for the same initiative
- Request frequent and detailed progress reports on initiatives
- Enforce compliance with specified requirements for business activities
- Require and review reporting for decisions from below
- Spend time with senior managers
- Create a safe environment for learning
- Explain the strategy clearly
- Empower frontline managers to stretch themselves
- Coach people

To-be Leadership Canvas

Frontline managers: Serve customers, not the boss

Current activities of BRG's frontline leaders vs. the activities employees think they should be doing:

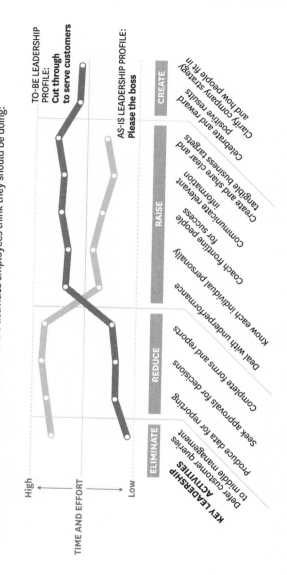

TO-BE LEADERSHIP PROFILE:
Cut through to serve customers

AS-IS LEADERSHIP PROFILE:
Please the boss

TIME AND EFFORT

High

Low

ELIMINATE	REDUCE	RAISE	CREATE

KEY LEADERSHIP ACTIVITIES

- Defer customer queries to middle management
- Produce data for reporting
- Seek approvals for decisions
- Complete forms and reports
- Deal with underperformance
- Know each individual personally
- Coach frontline people for success
- Communicate relevant information
- Create and share clear and tangible business targets
- Celebrate and reward positive results
- Clarify company strategy and how people fit in

To-be Leadership Canvas

Middle managers: More coaching, less control

Current activities of BRG's midlevel leaders vs. the activities employees think they should be doing:

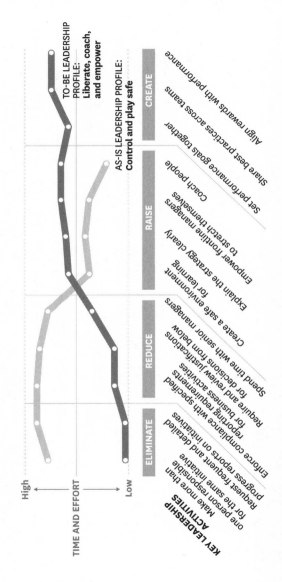

TO-BE LEADERSHIP PROFILE: **Liberate, coach, and empower**

AS-IS LEADERSHIP PROFILE: **Control and play safe**

TIME AND EFFORT — High ↕ Low

KEY LEADERSHIP ACTIVITIES

ELIMINATE
- Make more than one person responsible for the same initiative
- Request frequent progress reports on initiatives
- Enforce compliance with specified and detailed reporting requirements for business activities
- Require and review justifications for decisions from below

REDUCE
- Spend time with senior managers
- Create a safe environment for learning

RAISE
- Explain the strategy clearly
- Empower frontline managers to stretch themselves
- Coach people
- Set performance goals together

CREATE
- Share best practices across teams
- Align rewards with performance

To-be Leadership Canvas

Senior managers: From the day-to-day to the big picture

Current activities of BRG's senior managers vs. the activities employees think they should be doing:

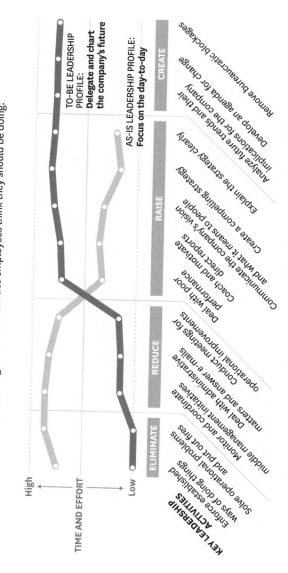

ABOUT THE AUTHORS

W. Chan Kim and *Renée Mauborgne* are professors at INSEAD, the world's second-largest business school, and codirectors of the INSEAD Blue Ocean Strategy Institute. They are the authors of *Blue Ocean Strategy*, which is recognized as one of the most iconic and impactful strategy books ever written. The theory of blue ocean strategy has been actively embraced by companies, governments, and nonprofits across the globe and is currently being taught in more than eighteen hundred universities around the world. *Blue Ocean Strategy* is a best-seller across five continents. It has sold over 3.6 million copies and has been published in a record-breaking 44 languages. Kim and Mauborgne are ranked in the top three of the Thinkers50 global list of top management thinkers and were named among the world's top five best business school professors by MBA Rankings. They have received numerous academic and management awards around the globe, including the Nobels Colloquia Prize for Leadership on Business and Economic Thinking, the Carl S. Sloane Award by the Association of Management Consulting Firms, the Leadership Hall of Fame by *Fast Company* magazine, and the

Eldridge Haynes Prize by the Academy of International Business, among others. Kim and Mauborgne are Fellows of the World Economic Forum in Davos. Mauborgne is a member of President Barack Obama's Board of Advisors on Historically Black Colleges and Universities (HBCUs). Kim is an advisory member for the European Union and is an advisor for several countries.

ALSO BY THESE AUTHORS

Harvard Business Review Press Books

Blue Ocean Strategy, Expanded Edition: How to Create Uncontested Market Space and Make the Competition Irrelevant

The W. Chan Kim and Renée Mauborgne Blue Ocean Strategy Reader

Harvard Business Review Articles

"Blue Ocean Strategy"

"Charting Your Company's Future"

"Creating New Market Space"

"Fair Process: Managing in the Knowledge Economy"

"How Strategy Shapes Structure"

"Knowing a Winning Business Idea When You See One"

"Red Ocean Traps"

"Tipping Point Leadership"

"Value Innovation: The Strategic Logic of High Growth"

Article Summary

Idea in Brief

The Problem

According to Gallup, only 30% of employees actively apply their talent and energy to move their organizations forward. Fifty percent are just putting their time in, while the remaining 20% act out their discontent in counterproductive ways. Gallup estimates that the 20% group alone costs the US economy around half a trillion dollars each year. A main cause of employee disengagement is poor leadership, Gallup says.

The Solution

A new approach called blue ocean leadership can release the sea of unexploited talent and energy in organizations. It involves a four-step process that allows leaders to gain a clear understanding of just what changes it would take to bring out the best in their people, while conserving their most precious resource: time. An analytic tool, the Leadership Canvas, shows leaders what activities they need to eliminate, reduce, raise, and create to convert disengaged employees into engaged ones.

Case in Point

A British retail group applied blue ocean leadership to redefine what effectiveness meant for frontline, midlevel, and senior leaders. The impact was significant. On the front line, for example, employee turnover dropped from about 40% to 11% in the first year, reducing recruitment and training costs by 50%. Factoring in reduced absenteeism, the group saved more than $50 million in the first year, while customer satisfaction scores climbed by over 30%.

CREATE UNCONTESTED MARKET SPACE AND MAKE THE COMPETITION IRRELEVANT

If you enjoyed reading *Blue Ocean Leadership*, turn to this expanded edition of the landmark bestseller *Blue Ocean Strategy*, embraced by business leaders and organizations worldwide.

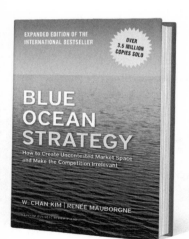

hbr.org/books

Invaluable insights
always at your fingertips

With an All-Access subscription to
Harvard Business Review, you'll get
so much more than a magazine.

Exclusive online content and tools
you can put to use today

My Library, your personal workspace for sharing,
saving, and organizing HBR.org articles and tools

Unlimited access to more than 4,000 articles in the
Harvard Business Review archive

Subscribe today at hbr.org/subnow

The most important management ideas all in one place.

We hope you enjoyed this book from *Harvard Business Review*. For the best ideas HBR has to offer turn to HBR's 10 Must Reads Boxed Set. From books on leadership and strategy to managing yourself and others, this 6-book collection delivers articles on the most essential business topics to help you succeed.

HBR's 10 Must Reads Series

The definitive collection of ideas and best practices on our most sought-after topics from the best minds in business.

- Change Management
- Collaboration
- Communication
- Emotional Intelligence
- Innovation
- Leadership
- Making Smart Decisions

- Managing Across Cultures
- Managing People
- Managing Yourself
- Strategic Marketing
- Strategy
- Teams
- The Essentials

hbr.org/mustreads

Buy for your team, clients, or event.
Visit hbr.org/bulksales for quantity discount rates.

Harvard
Business
Review
Press